D0354461

Victoria

Dear Grandmother

Recollections of Love

Dear Grandmother
Recollections of Love

HEARST BOOKS
NEW YORK

It is the policy of William Morrow and Company, Inc., and its imprints and affiliates, recognizing the importance of preserving what has been written, to print the books we publish on acid-free paper, and we exert our best efforts to that end.

ISBN: 0-688-15100-0

Library of Congress Cataloging-in-Publication Data available upon request.

Printed in Singapore
First Edition
10 9 8 7 6 5 4 3 2 1

For Victoria-
Nancy Lindemeyer, Editor-in-Chief
Susan Maher, Art Director
John Mack Carter, President, Hearst Magazine Enterprises

Edited by Linda Sunshine
Designed by Barbara Balch

Produced by Smallwood & Stewart, Inc., New York City

So many things we love are you,

I can't seem to explain except by little things,

but flowers and beautiful handmade things—

small stitches. So much of our reading and

thinking—so many sweet customs and so

much of our . . . well, our religion. It is all *you.*

I hadn't realized it before. This is so vague

but do you see a little, dear Grandma?

I want to thank you.

ANNE MORROW LINDBERGH
Bring Me a Unicorn

ℱOREWORD

𝒯hank goodness grandmothers come in so many delicious
varieties. For who among us would not want grandmothers picked
just for them. One of my grandmothers helped raise me, and how lucky
I was to have her every day for so many years. She made our home hum
with her energy and good cheer. Busy parents scurrying about the
world's business sometimes do not have the special touch that grandmothers offer. They seem to be able to peek into little hearts with
unique understanding.

With this book we honor the legions of grandmothers who have laps
to welcome tiny ones, soft shoulders for older children, open arms and
ears for all of us. Grandmothers enrich our lives because they are the
pillars that remind us that joys are to be cherished, and travails are not so
bad after all.

NANCY LINDEMEYER
Editor, Victoria

The past is a different country.
Somehow I had found my way back.

ROSAMUNDE PILCHER
Coming Home

She was my father's mother and had grown up in a family where good manners and proper clothes were esteemed above everything else. Early on she had rejected those values when she decided to study music and philosophy, wearing out-of-date clothing so she could afford books. She had more books than anyone I knew— leather-bound collections of poetry, thick volumes of philosophy, large books with prints of famous paintings, stacks of yellowed journals from her years of teaching philosophy at the university. Her hair, which had been red like my father's when she was younger, had turned white and she wore it in a braid around her head. . . . Though my parents had urged her several times to move in with us, she insisted on living alone in her Düsseldorf apartment. Many Saturday afternoons I visited her, and we'd listen to music that swelled through the rooms and roused feelings within me so powerful I couldn't name them; yet, the best of our moments together were tinged with my sadness that, soon, I'd have to leave her again.

URSULA HEGI
*Floating in My
Mother's Palm*

*D*uring that memorable summer, my grandmother's garden became an earthly paradise for me and the neighborhood children who gathered there each day. We frolicked among the cherry, apple, pear, fig, and plum trees, hid among the twisted scuppernong vines, and ran barefoot over the lush carpet of grass, squealing with delight as our suntanned bodies dodged the pelting spray of the water hose. We tried hard to avoid trampling where my grandmother's bright zinnias, marigolds, larkspurs, snapdragons, and roses reigned supreme. To quench our thirst on sweltering days, we chased the bell-clanging ice wagon down the street, catching the chips of ice that escaped. Our favorite spot in the garden was a far corner where the chinaberry tree stood. It offered refuge from the heat, provided low, sturdy branches for climbing, and yielded its gold-bronze berries as ammunition against enemies. On cool evenings, after supper, we huddled under the tree telling ghost stories. We captured lightning bugs in mason jars for our lanterns, and sometimes, at dusk, we strolled along the tree-lined walkways on the college campus, ending up at the ice cream store.

MARIE ELIZABETH DODSON
A Birthday Party

ALL MY ADULT life I've kept a picture near me of my grandmother at age four; she was one of those adults who knew how to connect with a child, and I, as the oldest grandchild, was able to absorb her memories in a way that made that little girl's face come alive. Big brown eyes, a bit of lace at her throat, an expression sober—as something so serious as a photograph in 1900 required—small reflections of that long-vanished little girl. That my little girls both have big brown eyes and serious faces seems like no accident to me, and I cherish these physical connections to someone they'll never know. *"Why, Kate looks just like her,"* marvels a visitor, peering at the old picture to compare children separated by 100 years. Sometimes I wonder about the long parade

of relatives vanished without my ever knowing who or what they were, and what remnant I carry all unknowing. There are so few traces from those times before photography, when resemblances were relegated to reminiscences. Even the clutch of daguerreotypes in a drawer that capture some of the Dallys of the 1840s, my great-great-grandfather among them, are like memory—faded, and flashing an image only when the light is right. . . .

Family resemblances are inescapable, as much a part of family life as, say, that recipe for vegetable soup and a tendency to weep noisily at sad movies, or the inevitability of glasses in the fifth grade. With an eye cocked for the gesture, the giggle, the blue eyes or the long feet, we tie up our tribe. What every family is confirming, of course, is continuity, and its own sense of self, the things that make the family circle a circle indeed.

CATHERINE CALVERT

A̶S OUR PARENTS HAD before us, we tried to go on making life as normal for our youngster as possible. And we delighted in the wonderful friends we were making and in the generosity and kindness of our neighbors. Buffalo may have been down on its luck in many ways, but the hearts of its people made it a place full of riches. Our neighbors took us in as if we were their own. Our child sat at the table of our over-the-back-fence friends, one rung down from their youngest child, as if he was a stair step. I often lifted him, bundled up to the tip of his nose, over the fence into safe and loving arms.

JENNY WALTON
Keep the Home Fires Burning

lived in my grandfather's country house attached to his silk factory, in a village in the hills of Veneto, with my mother and her family of women and old men: all the young men were at the war. We had moved here to escape the bombing in town. I was a pampered little girl, inquisitive, and always seeking adventure and magic. As a baby and then a toddler, and the only child in the household, I had everyone's attention and time. In those days of fear, I must have represented for them the hope for the future. In a world of doting adults, surrounded by their love and kindness, I grew up with great self-confidence.

KUKI GALLMAN, *I Dreamed of Africa*

THE HOUSE WHERE I WAS BORN

My mother-in-law—Mum—appeared with a tray of food such as made me wonder for a moment if she had mistaken me for a party of lumberjacks. As I greedily tucked into a delicious, steaming heap that brought to mind the Cairngorm Mountains re-created in comestible form, and afterward sat slumped with coffee and a happily distended stomach, we chattered away about this and that—the children, our impending move to the States, my work, her recent widowhood. Late in the evening—late, that is, for a couple of old-timers like us—she went into bustling mode again and, after making a great deal of industrious-sounding noise from every quarter of the house, announced that the guest room was ready. I found a neatly turned-down bed complete with hot-water bottle and, after the most cursory of ablutions, crawled gratefully into it, wondering why it is that the beds in the houses of grand-parents and in-laws are always so deliciously comfortable. I was asleep in moments.

BILL BRYSON
Notes from a Small Island

*F*LOWERS AND FOREIGN missions—her garden and the great kingdom of China; there was something unusual and touching about her preoccupations. Something quite charming, too. Women ought to be religious; faith was the natural fragrance of their minds. The more incredible the things they believed, the more lovely was the act of belief. To him the story of "Paradise Lost" was as mythical as the "Odyssey"; yet when his mother read it aloud to him, it was not only beautiful but true. A woman who didn't have holy thoughts about mysterious things far away would be prosaic and commonplace, like a man.

WILLA CATHER
One of Ours

Early spring was probably the most exciting time in the North Woods, for then Mother took us to hunt for May-basket flowers. On a chilly Saturday morning when the sun finally broke from gray skies into the thin clear sunshine of early spring, Mother hung an old willow basket over her arm and led my sister and me to a hidden entrance into the woods a half-mile away from our house.  Down a winding path, barely visible under the last patches of melting snow and moldy leaves, we followed Mother's sure steps, looking carefully as we walked for nearby flowers. Mother taught us how to find the delicate white Dutchman's-breeches and snowdrops and we gathered them into small bouquets with wild purple violets. . . . When we got home, we had hot rolls and cocoa while we constructed little baskets out of colored paper to fill with flowers and leave at our neighbors' doors.

SUSAN ALLEN TOTH
Blooming: A Small-Town Girlhood

TO MAKE *Syrop* OF

❀ VIOLETS ❀

First, gather a great quantity of violet flowers and pick them clean from the stalks and set them on the fire and put to them so much rose water as you think good. Then let them boil all together untill the colour be forth of them, then take them off the fire and strain them through a fine cloth, then put so much sugar to them as you think good, then set it againe to the fire until it be somewhat thick and put it into a violet glasse.

from THE GOOD HOUSE
WIFE'S JEWELL (1585)

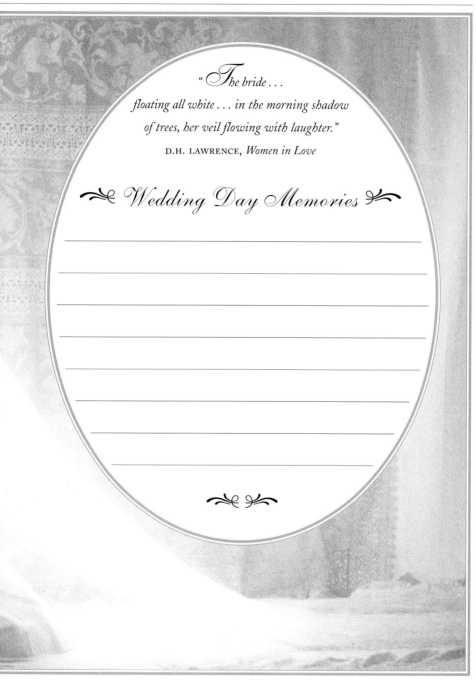

" *The bride . . .*
floating all white . . . in the morning shadow
of trees, her veil flowing with laughter."

D.H. LAWRENCE, *Women in Love*

Wedding Day Memories

Summer scents came up from the meadows; flies buzzed; the sun made the river glitter and heated the slates. Mère Simon came back into the room and fell softly asleep. She woke at the noise of the bells; the people were coming out from vespers.

GUSTAVE FLAUBERT
A Simple Heart

She walks among the loveliness she made,

Between the apple-blossom and the water—

She walks among the patterned pied brocade,

Each flower her son,

and every tree her daughter.

VITA SACKVILLE-WEST

This is my letter to the world,

That never wrote to me,—

The simple news that Nature told,

With tender majesty.

Her message is committed

To hands I cannot see;

For love of her, sweet countrymen,

judge tenderly of me!

EMILY DICKINSON

*T*hat first summer Reed and I spent in Europe after the war, Elsa invited us to an extraordinary evening in the south of France. We motored through Provence to Antibes. Ah!

the light of Provence! We were having a sort of love affair with France, seeing again all the beauty we'd loved so much all our lives, smelling all the wonderful smells . . . little bluebells, little Persian pinks, and all the other delicious smells of Provence. We spent the nights in such luxury on real linen sheets in the most divine *auberges* after wonderful dinners and walks after dinner under the pines. . . . Then we arrived in Antibes. . . . It was the year of *"La Vie en rose."* We'd go to bed rather early every night at the Hôtel du Cap, and we'd hear people walking home—everyone singing *"La Vie en rose."* Songs last forever. They fix particular years in your mind. That year, everyone was singing that song to everyone else into the night, and we'd lie there and listen to the happiness . . . it was all *"La Vie en rose."* The air is so still there. It holds music. Do you know what I mean?

DIANA VREELAND
D. V.

Lily was watching the men at work on the bridge, with her childish delight in a spectacle of any kind, when her grandmother addressed her.

"Guess I'll let you go down to the store an' git some salt, Lily," said she.

The girl turned uncomprehending eyes upon her grandmother at the sound of her voice. She had been filled with one of the innocent reveries of childhood. Lily had in her the making of an artist or a poet. Her prolonged childhood went to prove it, and also her retrospective eyes, as clear and blue as blue light itself, which seemed to see past all that she looked upon. She had not come to the old Barry family for nothing. The best of the strain was in her, along with the splendid stanchness in humble lines which she had acquired from her grandmother.

MARY WILKINS FREEMAN
Old Woman Magoun

My Grandmother is waiting for me to come home.
We live with walnuts and apples
in a one-room kitchenette above The
Same Day Liquor Gardens.

My Grandmother sits in a red rocking chair
waiting for me
to open the door with my key.

She is Black and glossy like coal.

We eat walnuts and apples,
drink root beer in cups that are broken,
above The
Same Day Liquor Gardens.

I love my Grandmother.
She is wonderful to behold
with the glossy of her coal-colored skin.
She is warm wide and long.
She laughs and she Lingers.

GWENDOLYN BROOKS
Novelle / My Grandmother Is Waiting
for Me to Come Home

ℋere, she felt, putting the spoon down,

was the still space that lies about the heart of things,

where one could move or rest;

could wait now. . .

listening.

VIRGINIA WOOLF

*P*ETAL *N*OTEPAPER

◇✕◇ Fill a box three-quarters full with sheets of textured rice or petal paper. In between every 3 or 4 sheets, sprinkle a handful of freesia (or orange or viburnum flowers). ◇✕◇ You also can add sweet-smelling herb leaves, such as scented geranium or lemon verbena. Leave the box covered, check every few days for excess moisture, and after a month, remove the flowers. ◇✕◇

SHARON ACKLAND

Fermina Daza had put on a loose-fitting silk dress belted at the hip, a necklace of real pearls with six long, uneven loops, and high-heeled satin shoes that she wore only on very solemn occasions, for by now she was too old for such abuses.

Her stylish attire did not seem appropriate for a venerable grandmother, but it suited her figure—long-boned and still slender and erect, her resilient hands without a single age spot, her steel-blue hair bobbed on a slant at her cheek. Her clear almond eyes and her inborn haughtiness were all that were left to her from her wedding portrait, but what she had been deprived of by age she more than made up for in character and diligence. She felt very well: the time of iron corsets, bound waists, and bustles that exaggerated buttocks was receding into the past. Liberated bodies, breathing freely, showed themselves for what they were. Even at the age of seventy-two.

GABRIEL GARCÍA MÁRQUEZ
Love in the Time of Cholera

Her mind was like her room, in which lights advanced and retreated, came pirouetting and stepping delicately, . . . and then her whole being was suffused, like the room again, with a cloud of some profound knowledge. . . .

VIRGINIA WOOLF
The Lady in the Looking-Glass

The boudoir is the room in which small objects of art . . . show to their best advantage. No detail is wasted and all manner of delicate effects in wood-carving, marquetry, and other ornamentation . . . here acquire their full value.

EDITH WHARTON AND OGDEN CODMAN, JR.
The Decoration of Houses (1897)

My grandmother interrupted the million tasks of her household— soaps, pies, bread, doughnuts, canning, jam and jellymaking . . . to tend her flowers.

DONALD HALL
Old Roses and Birdsong

*The cultivation
of beautiful penmanship is a minor art,
like flower arranging or needlepoint.
Beautiful handwriting does not change the world;
it softens it, giving dignity to those occasions
when the only way to be human is
to take pen in hand. . . .*

$\mathscr{O}$ne of the treasures in our family archives is a letter written by a great-uncle to the widowed mother of the girl he hoped to marry. It was a delicate situation. He was a poor cleric whose heart was larger than his prospects. *"My love,"* he admitted to his potential mother-in-law in a letter on thin rectory stationary, *"is my only plea."* But who could resist such a plea, written in even, blot-free penmanship, that ended with, *"There would be nothing lacking in the ful-filling of my cup of blessing could I but know that the desire of my heart would bring joy and peace to yours."* He got the girl.

PHYLLIS THEROUX
The Rewards of Penmanship

> *Please never stop writing me letters—they always manage to make me feel like my higher self.* ELIZABETH BISHOP

~*Special Friends*~

Thanksgiving was celebrated by the gathering of family and relatives from near and far around a great feast of good things. Of course people went to church Thanksgiving morning, but that was not what impressed a child. For days before, the house was astir with the many activities of preparation. Pies had to be made in quantity—mince, pumpkin, and apple-tart. My grandmother sometimes made forty. Those not used were stored in a cold room for future use.

The turkey, one or more, had to be prepared, but the crowning glory of the feast was the chicken pie. The huge dish was covered with a pie-crust, and a "sheaf of wheat" made of the crust decorated the top. There was always more anxiety that the chicken pie be baked just right than for anything else. Of course there were interesting jobs for little girls to do, such as sticking raisins in the mince pies, putting a stamp on them, etc., or [cutting] trees and fruit to decorate the tart pies. The feast always ended with nuts and raisins. After dinner there were always games, in which old and young joined.

from A MEMOIR WRITTEN FOR THE GLASTONBURY,
CONNECTICUT, HISTORICAL SOCIETY

At the time I was a boy of twelve, at home from school for the holidays. ❧ My mother's mother, Grandmamma Parrett, still lived in the house in West Twenty-third Street which Grandpapa had built in his pioneering youth, in days when people shuddered at the perils of living north of Union Square—days that Grandmamma and my parents looked back to with a joking incredulity as the years passed and the new houses advanced steadily Park-ward, outstripping the Thirtieth Streets, taking the Reservoir at a bound, and leaving us in what, in my school-days, was already a dullish back-water between Aristocracy to the south and Money to the north. ❧ Even then fashion moved quickly in New York, and my infantile memory barely reached back to the time when Grandmamma, in lace lappets and creaking *"moiré,"* used to receive on New Year's Day, supported by her handsome married daughters.

EDITH WHARTON
Old New York

*M*ake me thy lyre,

even as the forest is:

What if the leaves are falling like its own!

PERCY BYSSHE SHELLEY

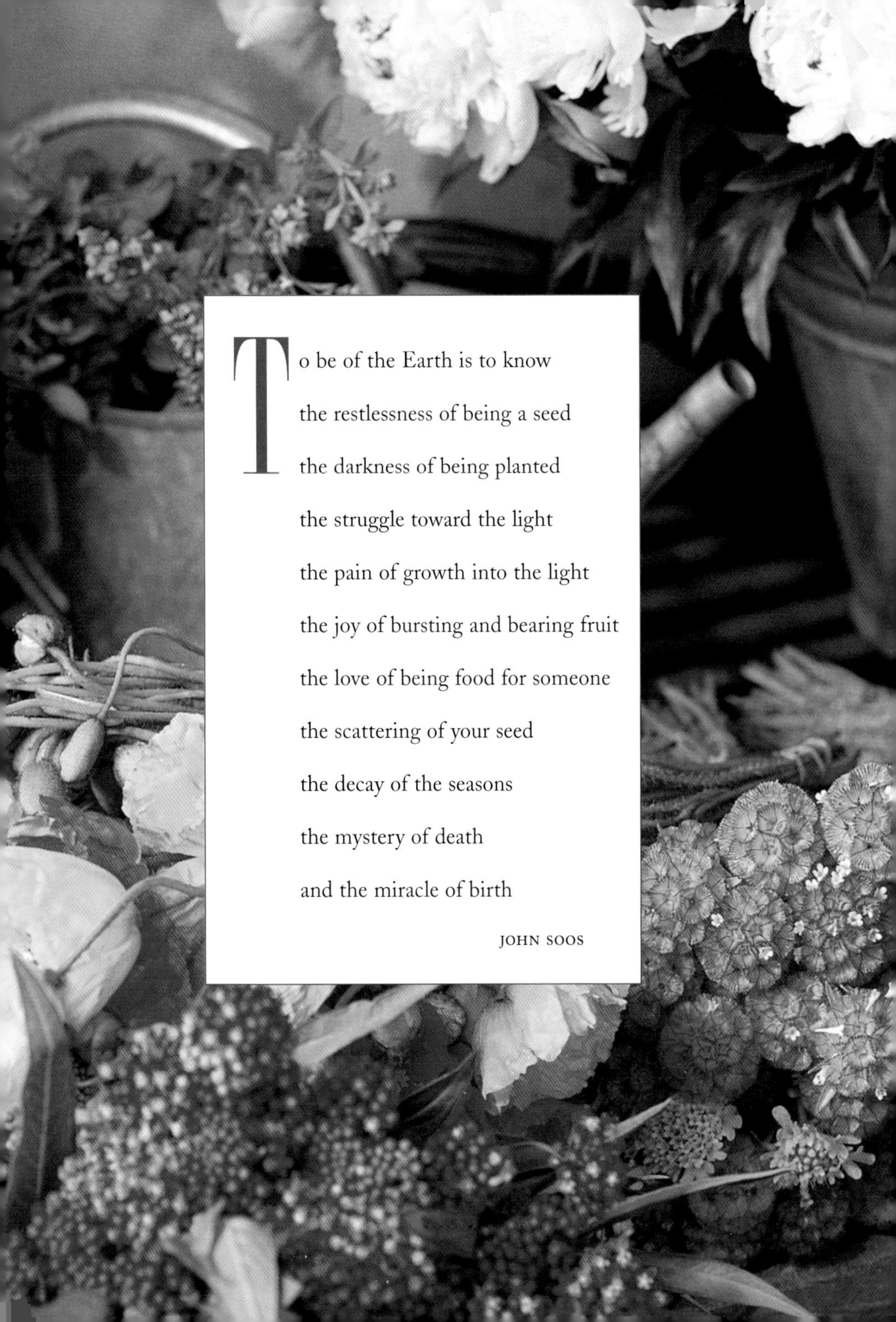

To be of the Earth is to know

the restlessness of being a seed

the darkness of being planted

the struggle toward the light

the pain of growth into the light

the joy of bursting and bearing fruit

the love of being food for someone

the scattering of your seed

the decay of the seasons

the mystery of death

and the miracle of birth

JOHN SOOS

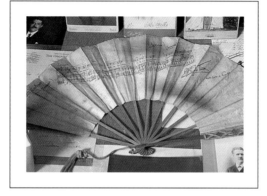

I HAVE TWO younger brothers. The older one, Benjamin Hale, who was born in 1948 when I was five years old, is named after our great-great-grandfather, a ship captain in the China trade who sailed out of Newburyport in the 1700s. ❀ My mother has special shelves filled with the blue and white Canton china that Benjamin Hale brought back as ballast from the Orient. ❀ A Chinese fan of his is framed in the upper hallway of my parents' house in Ossining, and a tiny pair of wire-rimmed spectacles in a lacquered case is kept in my grandmother's sewing box, which sits on a desk in the upstairs library.

SUSAN CHEEVER
Home Before Dark

$\mathcal{L}$OOK AT THE CHAIR on which your friend is sitting, at the carpet beneath your feet, at the paper on the walls, at the curtains which shut out the wintry landscape, at the table near you, at the clock, the candlesticks, nay, the very fire-irons—or it may be the iron mouldings upon your stove—at the picture-frames, the book-case, the table-covers, the work-box, the inkstand, in short, all of the trifling knick-knacks in the room, and on all these you may see, in bolder or fainter lines, a thousand proofs of the debt we owe to the vegetable world, not only for so many of the fabrics themselves, but also for the beautiful forms, and colors, and ornaments we seek to imitate. Branches and stems, leaves and tendrils, flowers and fruits, nuts and berries, are everywhere the models. . . . The most durable and costly materials the earth holds in her bosom, stone and marble, gold, silver, and gems, have been made to assume, in a thousand imposing or graceful forms, the lines of the living vegetation. How many of the proudest works of art would be wanting, if there had been no grace and dignity in trees, no beauty in leaves and flowers!

SUSAN FENIMORE COOPER
Rural Hours by a Lady (1854)

$\mathcal{W}$e came from a long line of doll lovers: My grand-mother still had her china-headed doll, the star of Christmas 1902, tucked in a drawer, and the only time I saw my mother cry was when I dropped and broke her Bye-lo baby, the much-pined-for present of her seventh year. So we had families of dolls, platoons of dolls, sorted by size and type, and each with as emphatic a personality as our own. . . .

We mothered our dolls, as our mother mothered us, weaving her secure background for us as she worked just out of earshot, making something cinnamony, perhaps, or bent at her own sewing task, turning out another superior example of doll couture.

CATHERINE CALVERT, *Our Mother's Daughters*

*O*ne day when the bluebells were in bloom I wrote the following. *I do not think I have ever seen anything more beautiful than the bluebell I have been looking at. I know the beauty of our Lord by it. It is strength and grace, like an ash. The head is strongly drawn over and arched down like a cutwater. The lines of the bells strike and overlie this, rayed but not symmetrically, some lie parallel. They look steely against paper, the shades lying between the bells and behind the cockled petal-ends and nursing up the precision of their distinctness, the petal-ends themselves being delicately lit. Then there is the straightness of the trumpets in the bells softened by the slight entasis and the square splay of the mouth.*

GERARD MANLEY HOPKINS
from a diary entry of 1870

$\mathscr{T}$HE EXCHANGE OF SEEDS and plants which always attends such garden visits is one of the pleasant incidents connected with them. My garden is a veritable album, and as I wander over our place I find many a dear friend or happy hour commemorated in it. This little clump of oxalis, naturalized so prettily in the woods, was gathered one lovely day when a merry party joined us in an expedition to the Profile Notch. That group of lady's-slippers came from the woods of a dear friend in Vermont. Here are moss roses from a magnificent rose garden in Massachusetts, and there are seedlings from the home of Longfellow, or willows rooted from cuttings brought from the South by Frederick Law Olmsted. Hardly a flower-loving friend have I who has not left an autograph in plant, or shrub, or tree in my garden, and in like manner many a thrifty plant has left my borders for those of distant friends.

ROSE FAY THOMAS
Our Mountain Garden

Is it so small a thing
To have enjoyed the sun,
To have lived light in the spring.

MATTHEW ARNOLD

$\mathcal{O}$*n the third floor* there was a sort of arched passage, connecting the two sides of the house, which Isabel and her sisters used in their childhood to call the tunnel and which, though it was short and well-lighted, always seemed to the girl to be strange and lonely, especially on winter afternoons.   She had been in the house, at different periods, as a child; in those days her grandmother lived there. Then there had been an absence of ten years, followed by a return to Albany before her father's death. Her grandmother, old Mrs. Archer, had exercised, chiefly within the limits of the family, a large hospitality in the early period, and the little girls often spent weeks under her roof—weeks of which Isabel had the happiest memory. The manner of life was different from that of her own home—larger, more plentiful, practically more festal; the discipline of the nursery was delightfully vague and the opportunity of listening to the conversation of one's elders (which with Isabel was a highly-valued pleasure) almost unbounded. There was a constant coming and going; her grandmother's sons and daughters and their children appeared to be in the enjoyment of standing invitations to arrive and remain, so that the house offered to a certain extent the appearance of a bustling provincial inn kept by a gentle old landlady who sighed a great deal and never presented a bill. Isabel of course knew nothing about bills; but even as a child she thought her grandmother's home romantic. There was a covered piazza behind it, furnished with a swing which was a source of tremulous interest; and beyond this was a long garden, sloping down to the stable and containing peach-trees of barely credible familiarity. Isabel had stayed with her grandmother at various seasons, but somehow all her visits had a flavour of peaches. HENRY JAMES, *Portrait of a Lady* (1881)

The PLEASURES of TEA

❦

✢ LOVELY LAVENDER TEA ✢

4 teaspoons orange-pekoe tea

3 fresh lavender flower heads or

⅓ teaspoon dried lavender flowers

Lavender honey to sweeten

❦

✢ SPICY ROSE TEA ✢

4 teaspoons orange-pekoe tea

1 tablespoon fresh rose petals or

1 teaspoon dried rose petals

½ teaspoon cinnamon stick chips

❦

❦ TIPS FOR THE ❦
P e r f e c t   C u p

WHETHER YOU ARE MAKING plain tea or an herbal blend, begin by taking the chill off your teapot: Pour some boiling water into it, swish it around for a minute or so, and pour it out. Then add the tea, whether loose or in bags, and after that the herbs and flowers, crushing their leaves and petals gently to release the flavorful oils. Pour in boiling water (use one cup water per one tablespoon of herbs), put on the lid, and cover the pot with a tea cozy if possible. Allow the tea to brew for five minutes; steeping it too long may produce a bitter taste.

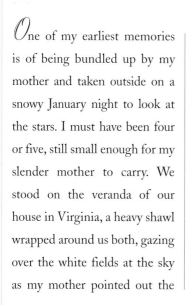

One of my earliest memories is of being bundled up by my mother and taken outside on a snowy January night to look at the stars. I must have been four or five, still small enough for my slender mother to carry. We stood on the veranda of our house in Virginia, a heavy shawl wrapped around us both, gazing over the white fields at the sky as my mother pointed out the constellations she knew. *"The North Star is the brightest star in the sky,"* she whispered, her warm breath wreathing my ear. *"Once you find it, you can always figure out where you are."* Nestled against my mother, I found this instruction both sensible and enchanting, and I have never forgotten it.

SUZANNE BERNE
Perfect Mornings, Perfect Memories

Grandfather,
Look at our brokenness.

We know that in all creation
Only the human family
Has strayed from the Sacred Way.

We know that we are the ones
Who are divided
And we are the ones
Who must come back together
To walk in the Sacred Way.

Grandfather,
Sacred One,
Teach us love, compassion, and honor
That we may heal the earth
And heal each other.

OJIBWAY PRAYER

THE FEAST WAS a noble feast, as has already been said. There was an elegant ingenuity displayed in the form of pies which delighted my heart. Once acknowledged that an American pie is far to be preferred to its humble ancestor, the English tart, and it is joyful to be assured at a Bowden reunion that invention has not yet failed. Beside a delightful variety of material the decorations went beyond all my former experience; dates and names were wrought in lines of pastry and frosting on the tops. There was even more elaborate reading matter on an excellent early-apple pie which we began to share and eat, precept upon precept. Mrs. Todd helped me generously to the whole word *Bowden*, and consumed *Reunion* herself, save an undecipherable fragment; but the most renowned essay in cookery on the tables was a model of the old Bowden house made of durable gingerbread, with all

the windows and doors in the right places, and sprigs of genuine lilac set at the front. It must have been baked in sections, in one of the last of the great brick ovens, and fastened together on the morning of the day. There was a general sigh when this fell into ruin at the feast's end, and it was shared by a great part of the assembly, not without seriousness, and as if it were a pledge and token of loyalty. I met the maker of the gingerbread house, which had called up lively remembrances of a childish story. She had the gleaming eye of an enthusiast and a look of high ideals.

"I could just as well have made it all of frosted cake," she said, "but 't wouldn't have been the right shade; the old house, as you observe, was never painted, and I concluded that plain gingerbread would represent it best. It wasn't all I expected it would be," she said sadly, as many an artist had said before her of his work.

SARAH ORNE JEWETT
The Country of the Pointed Firs

*W*HEN YOU ARE GETTING on in years it is nice to sit by the fire and drink a cup of tea and listen to the school bell sounding dinner, call-over, prep, and lights-out. ✍ Chips always wound up the clock after that last bell; then he put the wire guard in front of the fire, turned out the gas, and carried a detective novel to bed. ✍ Rarely did he read more than a page of it before sleep came swiftly and peacefully, more like a mystic intensifying of perception than any changeful entrance into another world. ✍ For his days and nights were equally full of dreaming.

JAMES HILTON
Good-bye, Mr. Chips

THE HEART OF the L-shaped, clapboard house was (and still is) the large, square kitchen, with its rocking chairs and oilcloth-covered dining table. In front of the chimney crouched the newfangled iron range, an invention of the 1820s that had displaced the fireplace for cooking and thrown American housewives into a tizzy as they learned to cope with this fire-breathing monster. Often the only way to determine whether an oven was hot enough to bake a loaf of bread or a cake was for the cook to thrust her hand inside and hold it there. . . .

My great-grandmother fed her husband, four daughters, and the men my great-grandfather hired to help him with his chores. The dinner horn she used for calling the workers in from the fields still sits upright in the kitchen cupboard and, when blown, gives forth with the loudest (and rudest) of blats.

DALE MACKENZIE BROWN
Nothing Fancy, Everything Good

The best thing about the stove was the warming oven. It was the first place we grandchildren checked upon arrival. There were always leftovers of some kind there, and *we* could *eat* them! Best of all was a biscuit. Grandma's biscuits were as big as our hands. She didn't cut them, she pinched off a handful of dough and patted and shaped it like a small loaf. Nobody's biscuits tasted like Grandma's. Sometimes there would be leftover bacon, thick and tasty, or home-cured ham. *So good!* And I never went home from Grandma's that she didn't send me with a quart jar of her home-canned pickled peaches, dill pickles, kraut, or a jar of wild plum jelly. Those were my favorites, and I felt she made them just for me.

MARTHA KEZER MERIDETH
Grandma Brook

GARNISHES

When my parents were married in Arles, my Grandmother Athalie took up pen and ink and wrote down a collection of her own mother's best recipes in a little blue notebook. I have that notebook in front of me now.

MICHEL BIEHN
Recipes from a Provençal Kitchen

Treasured Family Recipes

One could not live without delicacy, but when
I think of love I think of the big, clumsy-looking
hands of my grandmother, each knuckle a knob,
stiff from the time it took for hard grasping,
with only my childhood's last moment for the soft touch.
And I think of love this August when I look
at the zinnias on my coffee table. Housebound
by a month-long heat wave, sick simply of summer,
nursed by the cooler's monotone of comfort,
I brought myself flowers, a sequence of multicolors.
How tough they are, how bent on holding their flagrant
freshness, how stubbornly in their last days instead
of fading they summon an even deeper hue
as if they intended to dry to everlasting,
and how suddenly, heavily, they hang their heads at the end.
. . . I have studied these blooms
who publish the fact that nothing is tentative
about love, have applauded their willingness to take
love's ultimate risk of being misapprehended.

MONA VAN DUYN
A Bouquet of Zinnias

AN *Infusion* OF *Summer*

FOR A *Sweet-Smelling Bath*

OF ALL THE WAYS TO ENJOY the pick of a garden, making infusions is one of the most delightful. It's easy, too, only requiring a large handful of fresh flowers—or 1 ounce of dried—and 2½ cups of water. (Though distilled or spring water is best, you may use water from the tap if you boil it first.) Steep the blossoms for 10 minutes, drain and voilà—a caressing beauty bath awaits. I prefer adding jasmine and orange-flower water when I want to dally in the tub, but as an end-of-the-day pick-me-up, I crave white roses with lavender and sprigs of ivy to heal a burn and relieve sun-parched skin.

SHARON ACKLAND
A Perfumer's Diary

*M*y grandmothers were strong.
They followed plows and bent to toil.
They moved through fields sowing seed.
They touched earth and grain grew.
They were full of sturdiness and singing.
My grandmothers were strong.

My grandmothers are full of memories
Smelling of soap and onions and wet clay
With veins rolling roughly over quick hands
They have many clean words to say.
My grandmothers were strong.
Why am I not as they?

MARGARET WALKER ALEXANDER
Lineage

*A*bove my mantel is a painting of a little girl with a seashell. As she holds it up to the light, the sun streams through, turning the smooth inner surface into a glowing pink satin. No matter what the season, the painting's sunlight fills my study with summer's brightness. 🍂 Looking at the painting, I remember the story of its creation. *The little girl is posing for her father, a painter. Her arms grow heavy, her neck aches, she longs to rest a bit.* "El, El, look into the shell," *her father murmurs, and she remembers what a privilege it is to pose for him, how sought-after his paintings are.*

"Just a bit longer," *he promises,* "and then we'll stop for tea." 🍂 Eleanor was my grandmother, and the painting—one that her father could not bear to part with—has been handed down through the generations. For as long as I can remember, the shell in the painting sat on my grandmother's desk. In the winter, when cold fog rolled in off the sea, she would hold it up to the lamp and its rosy sheen would fill her with summer's warmth once again. . . . 🍂 One year . . . on Christmas morning I opened my grandmother's present and saw, nestled in tissue paper, the delicate pink and white of her shell. I picked it up and held it to my ear, and there was the ocean, murmuring. Outside, snow was falling softly past the window, but in the shell, cupped in my hand, waves lapped on a summer shore. 🍂 This year I have a granddaughter of my own. Her birth heralds the beginning of a new generation. When she comes to visit, I shall hold the shell up to her ear and she will hear the sound that has always drawn the women of our family to the ocean. It is the sound of her own heart. 🍂

FAITH ANDREWS BEDFORD
My Grandmother's Shell

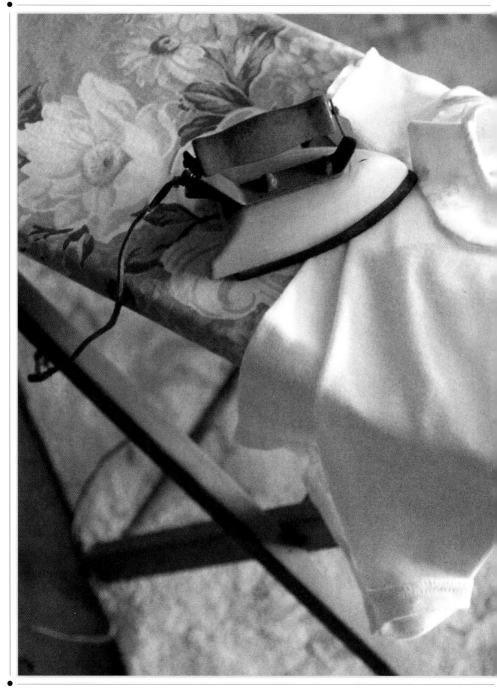

*T*he arrrival of a new generation
gives birth to the past, to the cycle of life,
the coming of each new season.
To this grandparent, it brings a clarity,
sharp, bittersweet, the panorama
of childhood memories—
of the generations that came before me,
grandparents, great-grandparents, and all
the tales of lives that preceded them.

DORIS BRYDEN RANDALL
The Dance of Life

$\mathcal{N}$obody sees a flower, really.
It is so small.
We haven't the time and
to see takes time,
like to have friends takes time.

GEORGIA O'KEEFFE

*M*y grandmother wrote in her notebooks that bore witness to life for fifty years. Smuggled out by certain friendly spirits, they miraculously escaped the infamous pyre in which so many other family papers perished. I have them here at my feet, bound with colored ribbons, divided according to events and not in chronological order, just as she arranged them before she left. Clara wrote them so they would help me now to reclaim the past and overcome terrors of my own.

ISABEL ALLENDE
The House of the Spirits

About My Grandmothers

I HAD ALWAYS ADMIRED her striking looks—the snow-white hair, the sapphire eyes, the brown skin, the perfectly molded features—and I reveled in her high, clear, precise articulation. Adeline made a little event of each idea in even a casual dialogue. She was in constant quest of the beautiful, in language, in friendship, in books, in the daily routine. She did not waste a scrap of life, which made my visits to her at tea-time oases in an urban existence where the very streets seemed gray with the litter of lost opportunities.

LOUIS AUCHINCLOSS, *The Book Class*

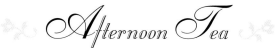

Afternoon Tea

*P*lease you, excuse me, good five-o'clock people,
I've lost my last hatful of words,
And my heart's in the wood up above the church steeple,
I'd rather have tea with the birds.

Gay Kate's stolen kisses, poor Barnaby's scars,
John's losses and Mary's gains,
Oh! what do they matter, my dears, to the stars
Or the glow-worms in the lanes!

I'd rather lie under the tall elm-trees,
With old rooks talking loud overhead,
To watch a red squirrel run over my knees,
Very still on my brackeny bed.

And wonder what feathers the wrens will be taking
For lining their nests next Spring;
Or why the tosses shadow of boughs in a great wind shaking
Is such a lovely thing.

CHARLOTTE MEW

*H*er flowers were exclusive blue.
No other color scheme would do.

Better than God she could reject
Being a gardener more select.

Blue, blue it was against the green
With nothing *not* blue sown or seen.

Yet secretly she half-confessed
With blue she was not wholly blessed.

All blues, she found, do not agree.
Blue riots in variety.

Purist-perfectionist at heart,
Her vision flew beyond her art—

Beyond her art, her touch, her power
To teach one blue to each blue flower.

ROBERT FRANCIS
Exclusive Blue

❧ *I*NCHFAWN WAS A SUMMER HOUSE that had been built in 1892. It was shingle, with white trim, and two round towers at the ends, each with a round window. Big-windowed, high-ceilinged, and large, it presumed an endless supply of servants and fuel. A deep porch ran along two sides of it, with a sloping, shingled roof, and broad steps led up to the front door from the circular driveway. Downstairs the rooms were large and pompous, and filled with dark, heavy oak, but upstairs furniture was simpler, white-painted wood and metal bedsteads, except in Granny's room, which held the beloved and funereal dark oak. The four big bedrooms on the second floor all had marble washstands with running water in them, but up on the third floor the bedrooms still had pitcher and ewer sets as they had when the house was built. Things had not been changed for decades. . . .

Laura loved Inchfawn; she loved its size, its shabby elegance, its presumptions, its permanence. ❧

ROXANA ROBINSON
Summer Light

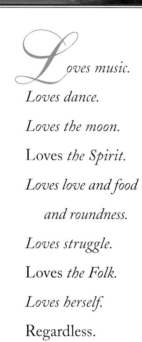

*L*oves music.

Loves dance.

Loves the moon.

Loves *the Spirit.*

Loves love and food

and roundness.

Loves struggle.

Loves *the Folk.*

Loves herself.

Regardless.

ALICE WALKER

Leisure

*W*hat is this life if, full of care,
We have no time to stand and stare.

No time to stand beneath the boughs
And stare as long as sheep or cows.

No time to see, when woods we pass,
Where squirrels hide their nuts in grass.

No time to see, in broad daylight,
Streams full of stars like skies at night.

No time to turn at Beauty's glance,
And watch her feet, how they can dance.

No time to wait till her mouth can
Enrich that smile her eyes began.

A Poor life this if, full of care,
We have no time to stand and stare.

W. H. DAVIES

 I never lived near my grandparents Ward, and so I don't imagine that my family celebrated Christmas at their house more than three or four times during my boyhood. But theirs was the definitive Christmas against which all others are still measured in my family. My grandparents' Christmas wasn't even particularly Christian so much as a celebration of family and abidance and continuity which, like Chanukah and all the irresistible festivals of light, induced in even their most irreligious descendants a hunger for ritual and remembrance. All Christmas morning long my grandfather's house used to breathe the sleepy steam of roasting turkey. As we opened our presents, one at a time in the dappled

glow of tree and hearth, Grandma's confections would already be circulating: almond crescents, addictive candied grapefruit rind, balls of chopped apricot rolled in sugar. . . . ❧ Grandpa was a man of firm culinary convictions: about the consistency of gravy, the buoyancy of boiled onions, the clarity of roasting juices. But truth be known, he was merely the figurehead: my grandmother was the steady driving piston of the Christmas kitchen engine: paring, chopping, sautéing, stewing: a juggler of eggs and mixer blades and any grandchildren who insisted on making themselves useful. . . . ❧ The wiring was poor in my grandparents' house, and so the light was dim and rosy, and even if it was not so dim and rosy it appears that way in the old slides Grandpa left behind as a proud record of his holiday productions. And so that is the glow my memory casts on all my holiday expectations, soft and hibernal and benign. ❧

ANDREW WARD, *The Christmas Feast*

I remember my grandfather, my *zaydie*, as a stern figure of authority, not very tall but quite good-looking. A white beard served as a frothy frame that set off his incredible blue eyes. His disarming smile gave him a roguish quality, but he possessed a temper that was known throughout the neighborhood and the surrounding towns.

My *bubbie* was a short woman with graying hair wound in a bun at the nape of her neck. A bit on the plump side, she always wore an apron around her ample waist. I can't recall a particular dress, only the apron. A

hint of lip rouge was the only makeup she wore to brighten her heart-shaped face. It seemed to me she was never without a book clutched in her hands. It annoyed her when she had to put the book down to complete her household chores.

SALLY BALER
Zaydie's Temper, Bubbie's Will

WHEN I WAS a first-grader, my family lived in Memphis, Tennessee, and my father used to take me to a museum called The Pink Palace. It was an unfinished mansion some wealthy man had commissioned to be built of smooth pink granite, one stone fitted carefully to the next, but the Depression or private ruin had wiped out his fortune and the unfinished estate became the property of the state, a museum for children. I can remember only one of its exhibits, which I loved: a large wall of little doors, arrayed from floor to ceiling, each with a tiny handle. Some I could reach myself, while my father would have to lift me to others. I must have worn him out with my desire to open and then close every single one of them. What was behind each door was a pane of glass, a window which gave onto a great—real?—tree, and each aperture revealed some different aspect of its life: nests, squirrels, spiders, stuffed birds whose glass eyes looked back with gleaming veracity. There was no way to ever see the entire tree at once, only the hundreds—were there?—of alternative perspectives the doors opened. This great curio cabinet, this museum of viewpoints, serves in my memory as a metaphor that resonates in many directions. The past itself seems to me like that tree, unseeable in its entirety, knowable only in its parts, each viewpoint yielding a different version of the story about what the whole might be.

What is the world but a tree too huge to see at once, known only through the shaping character of the particular aperture through which we see?

MARK DOTY, *Heaven's Coast*

It may not comfort you to know—
But if the time should ever come
When lily and delphinium
Are trampled to their doom
And only weeds are left to grow—

(Where has the gardener gone?
And who will mow the lawn?)

It may be comfort in your need
To find the goldenrod in bloom,
To find it flower and not weed.

ROBERT FRANCIS
It may not comfort you

$\mathcal{A}$ layer of ash several yards high covered the entire ranch. When Esperanza, my mother, returned from her wedding trip, all that she found under the remains of what had been the ranch was this cookbook, which she bequeathed to me when she died, and which tells in each of its recipes this story of a love interred.

They say that under those ashes every kind of life flourished, making this land the most fertile in the region.

Throughout my childhood I had the good fortune to savor the delicious fruits and vegetables that grew on that land. Eventually my mother had a little apartment building built there. My father Alex still lives in one of the apartments. Today he is going to come to my house to celebrate my birthday. That is why I am preparing Christmas Rolls, my favorite dish. My mama prepared them for me every year. My mama! . . . How wonderful the flavor, the aroma of her kitchen, her stories as she prepared the meal, her Christmas Rolls! I don't know why mine never turn out like hers, or why my tears flow so freely when I prepare them—perhaps I am as sensitive to onions as Tita, my great-aunt, who will go on living as long as there is someone who cooks her recipes.

LAURA ESQUIVEL
Like Water for Chocolate

It's all I have to bring today,

This, and my heart beside,

This, and my heart, and all the fields,

And all the meadows wide.

Be sure you count, should I forget,—

Some one the sum could tell,—

This, and my heart, and all the bees

Which in the clover dwell.

EMILY DICKINSON

$\mathcal{G}$iving is a form of dialogue and, at its most refined, of telepathy. The most memorable gifts seem to answer a question, settle a doubt, or anticipate a want the recipient perhaps hasn't yet thought of or been able to express. It's also a little mirror in which we see ourselves through the loving eyes of the giver. Once, at a particularly drab and melancholy moment of my life, a male friend gave me an unusual and lovely Spanish shawl, sumptuously embroidered with black flowers on fringed ivory silk. "*This looks like you. It feels like you,*" he wrote simply. His perception was as precious as the shawl itself, and I recover my original emotion—the surprise grace of his recognition— every time I wear it.

JUDITH THURMAN, *Playing Santa*

~*Flowers* are a delight to every one; to some, perhaps, merely for their beauty and fragrance; to others, independently of these acknowledged charms, for the varied pleasurable associations and thoughts they suggest. And foremost amongst these is the assurance they afford of the exuberant goodness of God. ~

REBECCA HAY
The Moral of Flowers (1833)

The autumn drifted away through all its

seasons. 🍂 The golden corn-harvest, the walks

through the stubble-fields, and rambles into

hazel-copses in search of nuts; 🍂 the stripping

of the apple-orchards of their ruddy fruit, amid

joyous cries and shouts of watching children;

🍂 and the gorgeous tulip-like colouring of the

later time had now come on with

the shortening days.

🍂

ELIZABETH GASKELL
Wives and Daughters (1864)

Our grandmother's name was Meta Waltenburger Doak. We children called her *Oma*, accenting both syllables. She was an imperious and kindhearted grande dame of  execrable taste, a tall, potbellied redhead, the proud descendant and heir of well-to-do Germans in Louisville, Kentucky, who boasted that she never worked a day in her life.

ANNIE DILLARD
An American Childhood

Once, in the small hours of the morning when I was wakeful, I listed in my mind the people I could call at two o'clock in the morning if I really needed to. And I was grateful that I could name more than a mere handful. And I thought, too, of the people who would call me. Unless there is an unexpected and terrible emergency, we don't act on this. But it is extraordinarily comforting to know that if there is a real need, there are people to whom we can reach out for help.

MADELEINE L'ENGLE, *Too Obvious to Forget*

TREASURED COMPANIONS

PERMISSIONS AND PHOTO CREDITS

Every effort has been made to trace the copyright owners. Please let us know if an error has been made, and we will endeavor to make necessary changes in subsequent editions.

Cover photographs: top left, Elyse Lewin; top middle, top right, and center, Toshi Otsuki; bottom left and bottom right, William P. Steele; bottom middle, Steve Randazzo.

1: Photograph by Wendi Schneider.

5: Photograph by Toshi Otsuki.

7: Photograph by Richard W. Brown. Excerpt from *Bring Me a Unicorn: Diaries and Letters of Anne Morrow Lindbergh, 1922-1928* by Anne M. Lindbergh, reprinted by permission of Harcourt Brace and Company.

9: Photograph by Starr Ockenga.

10: Photograph by William P. Steele.

12: Photograph by Starr Ockenga. Excerpt from *Floating in My Mother's Palm* by Ursula Hegi, copyright © 1991 by Ursula Hegi, reprinted by permission of Simon & Schuster.

13: Photograph by Wendi Schneider.

14: Photograph by Toshi Otsuki.

15: Photograph by Toshi Otsuki. Excerpt from "A Birthday Party" by Marie Elizabeth Dodson, which was included in *Legacie*s, edited by Maury Leibovitz and Linda Solomon, copyright © 1993 by The Jewish Association for Services to the Aged, reprinted by permission of HarperCollins Publishers, Inc.

16-17: Background photograph by Pierre Chanteau.

18: Photograph by William P. Steele.

19: Photography by Jana Taylor.

20: Excerpt from *I Dreamed of Africa* by

Kuki Gallman, copyright © 1991 by Kuki Gallman, reprinted by permission of Viking Penguin, a division of Penguin Books USA, Inc.

21: Photograph by Michael Skott.

22-23: Photograph by William P. Steele.

24: Photograph by Gross & Daley. Excerpt from *One of Ours* by Willa Cather, copyright © 1922 and 1950 by Willa Cather, reprinted by permission of Alfred A. Knopf, Inc.

25: Photograph by Kit Latham.

26: Photograph by Toshi Otsuki.

27: Photograph by Toshi Otsuki. Excerpt from *Blooming: A Small-Town Girlhood* by Susan Allen Toth, copyright © 1978 by Susan Allen Toth, reprinted by permission of the Aaron Priest Literary Agency.

28-29: Photograph by Toshi Otsuki.

30-31: Photograph by Tina Mucci.

32: Photograph by Toshi Otsuki.

34-37: Photographs by Toshi Otsuki.

38: Photograph by Toshi Otsuki. Excerpt from *D. V.* by Diana Vreeland, Alfred A. Knopf, Inc., 1984.

39: Photograph by Toshi Otsuki.

40-41: Photographs by Toshi Otsuki.

42: Photograph by Tina Mucci. "My Grandmother is Waiting for Me to Come Home" from *Children Coming Home* by Gwendolyn Brooks, copyright © 1991 by Gwendolyn Brooks, The David Co.

43: Photograph by Toshi Otsuki.

44: Photograph by Luciana Pampalone.

45: Photograph by Toshi Otsuki.

46-47: Inset photograph by Wendi Schneider. Background photograph by Luciana Pampalone. Excerpt from *Love in the Time of Cholera* by Gabriel García Márquez, translated by Edith Grossman, copyright © 1988 by Gabriel García Márquez, reprinted by permission of Alfred A. Knopf, Inc.

49: Photograph by Steve Ladner.

50: Photograph by Toshi Otsuki.

51: Photograph by William P. Steele.

52-53: Inset photograph by William P. Steele. Background photograph by Luciana Pampalone.

54-55: Photograph by Toshi Otsuki.

56: Photograph by William P. Steele.

57: Photograph by Jana Taylor.

59: Photograph by Wendi Schneider.

60-61: Photograph by Steve Cohen.

62: Photograph by Toshi Otsuki.

64: Photograph by Toshi Otsuki.

65: Photograph by Maurice Rougemont. Excerpt from *Home Before Dark* by Susan Cheever, copyright © 1984 by Susan Cheever, reprinted by permission of Houghton Mifflin Company, all rights reserved.

66: Photograph by Gross & Daley.

67: Photograph by Toshi Otsuki.

68-69: Inset photograph by Nana Watanabe. Background photograph by Toshi Otsuki.

70: Photograph by Tina Mucci.

71: Photograph by William P. Steele.

72: Photograph by Toshi Otsuki.

72-73: Photograph by Nic Barlow.

74: Photograph by Starr Ockenga.

75: Photograph by Toshi Otsuki.

76-77: Photograph by John Glover.

78: Photograph by Tina Mucci.

80: Photograph by Luciana Pampalone.

81: Photograph by William P. Steele.

82: Photograph by John Kane at Silver Sun Studios.

83: Photograph by Toshi Otsuki.

84-86: Photograph by Toshi Otsuki.

87: Photograph by Pierre Chanteau. Excerpt from *Good-bye, Mr. Chips* by James Hilton, copyright © 1962 by Alice Hilton, reprinted by permission of Little, Brown and Company.

88-89: Photograph by Chris Drake.

90: Photograph by Joshua Greene.

91: Photograph by Elyse Lewin. Excerpt from "Grandma Brook" by Martha Kezer Merideth, which was included in *Legacies*, edited by Maury Leibovitz and Linda Solomon, copyright © 1992 by The Jewish Association for Services to the Aged, reprinted by permission of HarperCollins Publishers, Inc.

92: Photograph by Luciana Pampalone.

94-95: Photograph by Toshi Otsuki. Excerpt from "A Bouquet of Zinnias" from *Near Changes* by Mona Van Duyn, copyright © 1990 by Mona Van Duyn, reprinted by permission of Alfred A. Knopf, Inc.

96: Photograph by Starr Ockenga.

97: Photograph by Jim Cooper.

Chris Drake. Excerpt from *Out Here* by Andrew Ward, reprinted by permission of Penguin Books USA, Inc.

120-121: Photographs by Toshi Otsuki. Excerpt from "Zaydie's Temper, Bubbie's Will" by Sally Baler, which was included in *Legacies*, edited by Maury Leibovitz and Linda Solomon, copyright © 1993 by The Jewish Association for Services to the Aged, reprinted by permission of HarperCollins Publishers, Inc.

122: Photograph by Toshi Otsuki.

123: Photograph by Jana Taylor. Excerpt from *Heaven's Coast* by Mark Doty, copyright © 1996 by Mark Doty, reprinted by permission of HarperCollins Publishers, Inc.

124-125: Photograph by Toshi Otsuki. "It May Not Comfort You" from *Robert Francis: Collected Poems, 1936–1976* by Robert Francis (Amherst: University of Massachusetts Press, 1976), copyright ©

1976 by Robert Francis.

126-127: Photograph by Starr Ockenga. Excerpt from *Like Water for Chocolate* by Laura Esquivel, copyright translation © 1992 by Doubleday, a division of Bantam Doubleday Dell Publishing Group Inc., reprinted by permission of Doubleday, a division of Bantam Doubleday Dell Publishing Group, Inc.

128: Photograph by Toshi Otsuki.

129: Photograph by Tina Mucci.

130: Photograph by Toshi Otsuki.

133: Photograph by Michael Skott.

134: Photograph by Toshi Otsuki.

135: Photograph by William P. Steele.

136: Photograph by Richard W. Brown.

144: Photograph by Wendi Schneider.